⌜SHOW-OFFS⌟

Created and Produced by Firecrest Books Ltd
in association with John Francis/Bernard Thornton Artists

Copyright © 1999 Firecrest Books Ltd
and Copyright © 1999 John Francis/Bernard Thornton Artists

Published by Tangerine Press™, an imprint of Scholastic Inc.
555 Broadway, New York, NY 10012

Tangerine Press™ and associated logo and design are trademarks of Scholastic Inc.

ISBN 0-439-15346-8

Printed and bound in Belgium
First printing December 1999

SHOW-OFFS

Bernard Stonehouse

Illustrated by
John Francis

TANGERINE PRESS™ and associated logo
and design are trademarks of Scholastic Inc.

For Joe

Art and Editorial Direction by
Peter Sackett

Designed by
Paul Richards, Designers & Partners

Edited by
Norman Barrett

Color separation by
Sang Choy International Pte. Ltd.
Singapore

Printed and bound by
Casterman, Belgium

Contents

Introduction LOOK AT ME

Every day, thousands of adults all over the world warn thousands of young people to stop showing off. This book is about animals that would not heed such a warning. All our subjects are show-offs and all show off madly as part of their everyday lives.

Throughout the animal kingdom generally, and even more so among plants, showing off is widespread. Many animals for many different reasons need to draw attention to themselves, in effect to shout: "I am important. Look at me." They don't always shout. They may sing from the treetops, wear bright colors, dance up and down, or emit clouds of perfume. Biologists call it "display," but that is just another name for showing off. Flowers show off all the time. Tell a rose not to show off, and you are missing an important point.

There have to be very good reasons for being a show-off. Another book in this series, called "Camouflage," stresses the lengths to which some animals go to hide themselves away. Some hide so that predators cannot find them. Others hide so they can jump out and be predators themselves. With so many predators around, who wins by showing off?

Displays have functions and advantages as well as dangers. Some help to hold communities together, as picturesque folk-dress unites villagers and unique uniforms unite armies. Others are essential for courtship.

Among animals, it is usually the males who posture and decorate themselves, and the females who select from among them. Some decorations, however, are simple warnings: "Touch me, and you'll regret it." Just a few are lies, as when harmless animals are dressed to look like more dangerous ones.

We like animals that show off. As we demonstrate here, showing off adds much to the interest and excitement of life. If hiding, camouflage, and dull uniformity were the only ways to live — if we all wore gray suits — what a dreary world it would be.

A male peacock feather with its spectacular "eye" design, one of hundreds shown when this bird displays his fan, or train.

— Rhinoceros hornbill WALLED IN

Hornbills are birds that live in Africa and southern Asia. They come in all sizes from 18 inches (45 cm) to 5 feet (1.5 m) tall. Several species have a "casque" – a plate or hollow tube on top of the bill. When a hen hornbill is ready to lay eggs, she and her mate find a hollow tree and then they wall her into it with mud, leaving just a narrow gap for air. She lays her eggs and incubates them for over a month, fed by the male. He feeds the chicks, too, until they are half grown and can safely be released into the world.

This rhinoceros hornbill, one of the bigger species, lives in the rain forests of Malaysia and Indonesia. His huge, upturned casque looks vaguely like a rhino's horn. It also looks immensely top-heavy, but is hollow and surprisingly light. The casque protects his eyes from twigs and branches, and is probably also an advertisement – an announcement that he is a fine male who is good at wall-building, and ready to take care of a hen properly. He feeds on nuts, fruit, and insects, poking the bill, with its long sausage-like tongue, through the tightly knit twigs of trees and bushes, selecting only the choice nuts and fruit from ripening bunches, and then rolling them back into his throat.

Lovely cotinga FINE FEATHERS

There are a dozen or more kinds of cotingas. The males, or cocks, are all brightly colored. Lovely cotinga cocks of Central America, in brilliant peacock-blue with black wings and a vivid purple-red breast, positively glow in the forest sunlight. Their hens, in darker, more down-to-earth plumage, merge with the background vegetation and the tree bark. During courtship, the males show off with a spectacular competition dance, flashing madly back and forth to attract the hens' attention. The hens view them critically, make their choices, and mate with whichever male they like. After this, the breeding is strictly the hens' concern. They build the nests, lay the eggs, and incubate them, while the cocks continue to exhibit themselves.

The males, in their brilliant plumage, are more likely to attract predators and be killed. Moralists would say they are paying the price of vanity. However, in drawing attention to themselves, they are also keeping predators away from their more vulnerable nesting hens. Does that make them blue-suited heroes, defending hearth and home? We do not know enough about cotingas to say, and wise biologists do not moralize. It is just one of many curious — but successful — ways of raising a family in the Central American jungle.

— Elephant seal A WARNING TRUNK

It is early spring, the start of the breeding season, and these two male elephant seals are rivals. In a few days' time, dozens of pregnant females will haul out onto the beaches to give birth. Two to three weeks later, the mothers will be ready to mate again.

"Beachmasters" — males big enough to defend a patch of beach from other males — will mate with the females on their patch, fathering next year's crop of pups. Except during the breeding season, male elephant seals get along well together. But as spring approaches, rivalries develop. Their noses grow into huge, overhanging trunks and, when rivals meet, both inflate their trunks and roar into them, magnifying the sound. Then they fight, often savagely. The winner holds the beach and his trunk deflates until the next challenger comes along.

The elephant seal facing us here is 20 feet (6 m) from nose to tail, about 15 years old, and fully grown. His rival (far left) is younger and slightly smaller. They are much bigger than the females (below).

Golden lion tamarin FEW LEFT

These tamarins, looking like cross miniature poodles, are South American monkeys from the rain forests of southern Brazil. About 1 foot (30 cm) long, with slightly longer furry tails, they are not easy to spot in the strong light and shade of the forest. You would have to look hard and be lucky to see one, as there are very few left. You would have to be even more fortunate to see these three different species together.

Tamarins scamper on small black paws along the branches, jumping and swinging like acrobats from branch to branch, with fur gleaming in the sunshine, lionlike manes shimmering. They move in small family groups, the male usually leading, the female following, with one or two babies clinging to her fur, and a couple of juveniles — last year's babies — close at hand. Chattering and squeaking, they munch ripe fruit and search for more. Occasionally they drop to the ground to find crickets and other insects, leaping into the trees at the first signs of danger.

The brilliant mane of the golden lion tamarin (middle) and the vivid black-and-white appearance of the cottontop (left) and the moustached tamarin (right) are show-off colors and patterns that make these little animals attractive to each other. Sadly, it also makes them attractive to humans. Thousands have been taken from the forests to be sold as pets. Now, a more serious danger affects all three species. Their forests are being cut for timber, and to clear the land for farming and building, leaving the tamarins homeless. The black-and-white species are rare, and only a few dozen wild golden lion tamarins remain free.

— Ring-tailed lemur BATTLE OF SCENTS

About 17 different kinds of lemurs live in the forests of Madagascar and the neighboring Comoro Islands, off the east coast of Africa. Related closely to monkeys, they live mainly on fruit, nuts, and insects. "Lemur" is Latin for "spirit of the night," and many are active only from dusk to dawn. But these ring-tailed lemurs walk by day.

Only ring-tailed lemurs have tails as bushy and elegantly striped as these. They move through the forest in troops of a dozen or more, including several adult males and females and their offspring. In a clearing on a bright, sunny day, you might see a gathering of ring-tailed lemurs, some sitting and watching, like this wide-eyed mother and daughter, while others stand with tails upright, waving them like banners.

Is it a beauty contest, to see which has the longest, the furriest, perhaps the most stripy tail? More probably it is a border dispute. Two troops or bands from neighboring territories have met, and each is asserting its claim by sending its own scents over the others. Before raising and waving their tails, the lemurs whisk them across scent glands on their arms, saturating them with distinctive musky smells. The waving tails spread the scents widely. Everyone gets the message, and everyone agrees. We are us, and they are them, and it is far too nice a day to fight. So mother and daughter lemur, with the rest of their troop, can go on their way in peace.

Birds of paradise BRILLIANT PLUMES

Birds of paradise, about the size of crows, live in New Guinea, northern Australia, and neighboring islands. When 16th-century explorers first brought specimens back to Europe, naturalists were struck by their beauty. They could only have come from paradise — hence the name. There are 40 or more species, some drab, others unbelievably colorful and "way-out." The more striking species were named for emperors and kings, and the one shown here is named for Count Raggis. Who was Count Raggis? We have forgotten, but his name lives on in this splendid bird.

Basically brown, with an orange-yellow hood and collar, green-brown chin, and blue-gray bill, it doesn't sound all that exciting. That is the male — the hen (lower down on the branch) is even duller. But when the male starts courting, with one or two hens lined up to watch, he throws himself into a crazy show-off dance, bowing, swinging from side to side, and ending in a flurry of brilliant orange or gold plumes like a well-timed conjuring trick.

Showing off has cost birds of paradise dearly. Hundreds of thousands have been killed to decorate native headdresses and clothing, and the hats of wealthy European and American women. Fortunately for the birds, their forests were difficult to penetrate, and so the supply was limited. And now that fashions have changed, the remaining birds of paradise can show off to each other in relative safety.

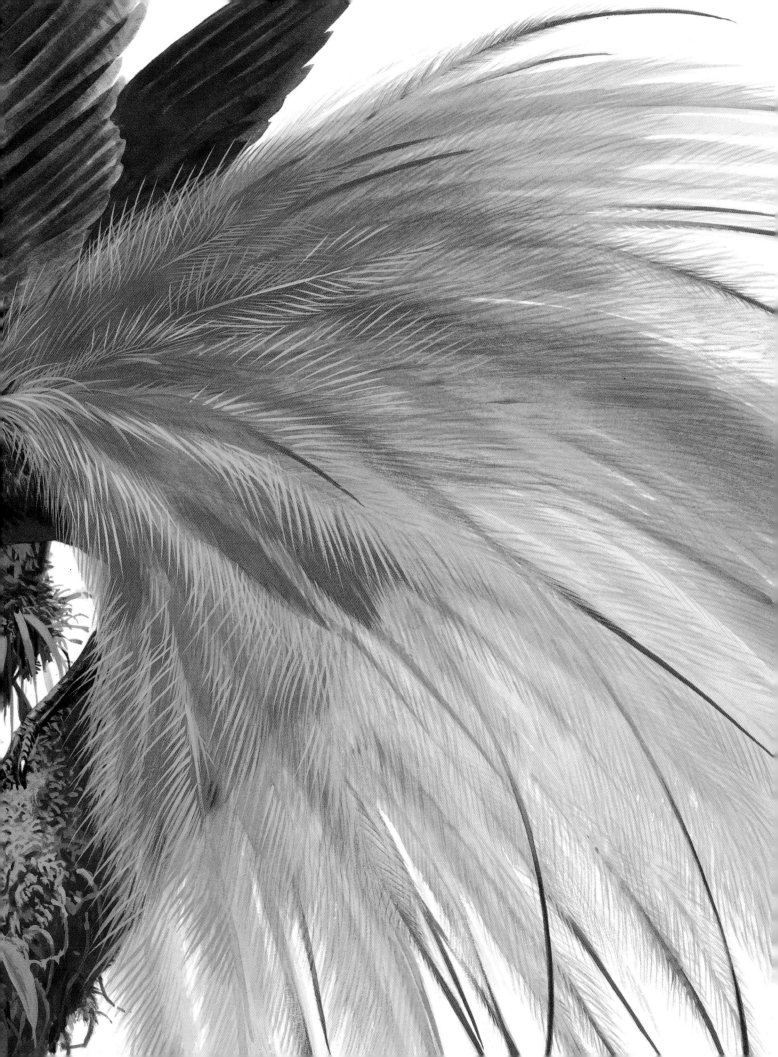

Mandrill A TOUCH OF COLOR

To the drab-green forests of equatorial west Africa, mandrills bring welcome color. Ground-dwelling monkeys, they feed on leaves, fruit, and insects. Males are bigger than females, weighing up to 55 pounds (25 kg). Young mandrills climb trees and leap from branch to branch like other small monkeys. Older ones, heavier and more sedate, stay closer to the ground.

They walk on all fours, with both hind legs and forelegs straight, and stubby tail pointing to the sky. Only the adult males are colorful, with a reddish-brown beard, crimson nose, and ridged sky-blue cheeks. The vivid blue of the cheeks is echoed in a bright blue backside, often with trimmings of violet and red. Why?

Mandrills live in small family troops, often made up of an adult male with two or three females and their young. Several troops may live and forage together. Only occasionally do quarrels arise, to be settled by displays among the leaders.

The leaders are the "big guys" with the red-and-blue faces and blue backsides. When the biggest big guy opens his mouth, curls back his upper lip, and exposes pink gums and huge canine teeth, smaller guys get the message. When the big guy turns and walks away, his backside glows like a light in the forest, and the smaller guys follow. What could be simpler?

Temminck's tragopan LIVELY DISPLAY

Tragopan was a mythical bird of Ethiopia, said to be horned like a goat. Now the name is given to five species of pheasants from India, China, and southeastern Asia — medium-sized, stocky birds of the mountain forest, with short round wings and whirring flight. They roost in trees, but forage mainly on the ground. Strong feet and toes scratch and turn over the soil, and the short bills peck for seeds, insects, and other small creatures. Tragopan males, or cocks, are vividly colored, with tufts of feathers over their eyes that might just be mistaken for horns; the hens are drab, in earth tones.

This Temminck's tragopan is the most colorful of all. But bright colors by themselves do not make a bird conspicuous. Stand this cock on a white kitchen table, and you will fully appreciate his gorgeous coloring. Turn him loose in a forest clearing, against a background of brown grass, dark twigs, and dead leaves, and the moment he stands still he will practically disappear. In strong light and shade, the cock matches his environment almost as closely as the hen.

To become a proper show-off and attract a female, he has to move in ways that are quite different from his ordinary, everyday movements of walking, scratching, and feeding. He has to do it on the ground — she will pay no attention if he takes off and flies. So he runs around his hen in a circle, with the near wing down like a banking aircraft, races toward her with horns and throat feathers raised, and dazzles her with shaking and quivering. It is hard work on a hot day, but it gets results.

Australian frilled lizard PUZZLING PREY

Here is a lizard some 30 inches (76 cm) long, from the sandy scrublands of northern Australia. It feeds on insects and spiders, eggs of ground-nesting birds, and other small food. During the heat of the day it rests, then becomes active again in the afternoon.

Most of the time it looks like any other pinkish, grayish, or green-brown lizard. When threatened, however, it spreads the rather messy-looking "scarf" around its neck and displays the frill. This is an unusual structure of thin scaly skin, sometimes brightly colored, supported on a half dozen strong, narrow hyoid bones extending backward from the tongue. As the frill spreads, the mouth opens wide, revealing a bright pink- or blue-and-yellow lining. At the same time, the lizard steps forward and hisses.

This is puzzling to predators that have never before met a frilled lizard. The creature that, just a second ago, was a slim, harmless-looking candidate for supper, has suddenly turned into a threatening monster. If it can shake an umbrella at you, flash colors, and shout "Szzzz," what else might it do? A wise predator looks elsewhere for its meal. The lizard then folds its frill and continues with the business of living.

Sulfur-breasted toucan BILLBOARD

Toucans live in the forests of South and Central America. In common with hornbills, they all seem to have bills that are much too big. This sulfur-breasted toucan, about 20 inches (50 cm) long from tip of bill to tip of tail, owes almost a quarter of its length to that enormous bill.

Thoughtful toucans probably wonder how smaller birds survive with their miserable, slender bills. Like hornbills, they find a long, conical bill just right for delving into bushes and picking out fruit and berries. Weight is no problem. Their bill is a masterpiece of engineering. Even sulfur-breasted toucans do not fall from their perches or fly head-down.

Why so much color? All toucans are colorful birds, but this particular species has black, white, red, and yellow on its body, and pink, yellow, and two shades of green on its face and bill. Surely this is excessive? Again, the colorful toucan has an answer. There are over 35 different kinds of toucans in South and Central America, with different species sharing the same habitats. To avoid interbreeding, it pays to be as different as possible. Three colors, six colors, what does it matter? And if you are blessed with a big bill, be thankful and make a billboard of it.

— Coral snake, milk snake MIMICRY

The average snake gliding quietly by wears drab, "merge-with-the-background" green and brown colors. Snakes that live in deserts, blotched and striped in conspicuous red, yellow, and black, are using a different strategy. For some reason it pays for them to be seen. Here are two snakes in these striking colors, at first glance so similar that they might be closely related, though in fact they are not. Some would say they are mimicking each other. The smaller one, an Arizona coral snake, has a bite that is poisonous to birds and small mammals, and may even kill humans. The larger Louisiana milk, or king, snake has no venom.

You have heard that one of the two is dangerous. So what do you do when you meet a snake that looks like one of these? You might kill it, to be safe either way. You might back away and leave it, which is kinder and less trouble. Either way, you treat the two alike because both wear bright colors. But does the harmless snake benefit from this? Wouldn't it be better off in drab green or brown, blending with its background instead of play-acting?

In this picture, the deadly coral snake is below; the larger one is the harmless milk snake. To be safe yourself, remember the rhyme, "Red against yellow, dangerous fellow." But keep away from both, in case they haven't heard it.

Ornate umbrella bird UMBRELLAS ON PARADE

Don't expect an umbrella bird to look like an umbrella. Closely related to the cotingas, they are 12-18 inches (30-45 cm) long from bill to tail, and live in highland forests of South and Central America. There are three species, more or less colorful. This male ornate umbrella bird, is elegant, in feathers of tasteful slate-gray. The highlight of his decoration is a feather-covered wattle hanging from the throat, like a gray necktie.

We know very little about the day-to-day life of these birds. Females of all the species are duller than the males, and almost certainly responsible for nest-building, incubation, and care of the young. But where is the umbrella? That takes the form of a crest on top of the head, which opens like a parasol or small plumed hat when the bird gets excited.

During courtship meetings, the males raise their umbrellas and dance from side to side, chattering and shaking their gray neckties. The hens, under smaller umbrellas, watch the males closely, perhaps comparing the size and splendor of their umbrellas. Maybe this is how ornate umbrella birds select their future mates, and keep their umbrellas in shape from one generation to the next.

Red-faced uakari GETTING A SUNTAN

Uakaris are monkeys of the Amazon rain forest, about 20 inches (50 cm) long, with a tail only 6 inches (15 cm) long — unusually short for a South American monkey. There are three species, one with a black face and two with red faces. This one, called the red, or red-faced, uakari, has the reddest face of all. Its coat too is reddish-brown, and long and shaggy, probably to keep the rain out.

We know little of them in the wild. They live in trees, feeding mainly on leaves and shoots, and move in troops of a dozen, sometimes in gatherings of a hundred or more. We have no idea why uakaris — again unusual among monkeys — are bald-headed and red-faced. They are said to turn paler if kept indoors, and to redden in the sun, suggesting that the color may be linked either with tanning or with keeping cool. We, too, turn red in the sun, though rarely so red as red-faced uakaris. The color is a show-off display of some kind, but we know not what.

They live quite happily in zoos, though they rarely breed in captivity. Whether happy or not, they have the misfortune to look uncannily like the most unhappy, most disagreeable people we know. But perhaps that misfortune is ours, not theirs.

Magnificent frigatebird RED BALLOON

Frigatebirds are large black or black-and-white birds of tropical oceans, light and kitelike, with pointed wings spanning over 6 feet 6 inches (2 m) and forked tails. They feed mainly on flying fish, which they catch in the air. This takes accuracy and skill, for the fish are airborne only for seconds at a time, and skim fast and low over the ocean surface. Frigatebirds also rob other seabirds of their prey. They fly up behind one and pull its tail or wing until the victim vomits up its recently caught fish, which the frigatebird catches in midair.

Magnificent frigatebirds nest in trees and shrubs on islands from the Galapagos to the Caribbean Sea and west Africa. Here is a male on its nest, looking for a mate. He has spread his wings and inflated a balloon of red skin in his throat, a display that attracts females flying overhead. A female has landed almost on top of him, and is considering the situation. It will not take long. In two or three weeks' time courtship will be over, the balloon deflated and forgotten, and the frigatebirds' world will center on their large white egg.

— Golden pheasant STATELY DANCE

Pheasant is a name given to several different kinds of ground-dwelling birds that are popular because of their beauty, and readily breed and interbreed in captivity. Cock, or male, pheasants of all kinds are brightly colored, hen pheasants more drab. This golden pheasant is one of the group called ruffed pheasants, which live in the mountains of western China, but are now common in aviaries and game parks all over the world. Ruffed pheasants have a broad neck collar, or ruff, and a crest on their heads, both of which come into action when they are displaying. Golden pheasant cocks are brilliant yellow-gold, barred with black and brown. Hens, too, have a little gold among their feathers, but are nowhere near as spectacular as their mates.

The cock's mating display is a stately dance with head down, wings spread, and long tail raised in the air. He performs to a harem of three or four hens, who seem indifferent but are usually sufficiently impressed to mate with him. Each hen scratches a nest, lays a dozen or more eggs, and incubates them for three to four weeks. All eggs in the nest hatch together. For two or three further weeks, unaided by their gorgeous husband, the hens lead their cheeping chicks in search of food.

Imperial angelfish SLIM AND BEAUTIFUL

You may see beautiful angelfish in a freshwater aquarium, but you will not see this kind. Imperial angelfish live in the sea, mostly among tropical coral reefs. A reef may support several species of marine angelfish and very similar — though not closely related — butterfish, most of them as bright and as different as parrots in a tropical forest.

Wedge-shaped fishes, they grow to 1 foot (30 cm) long from nose to tail, but only 1–2 inches (2.5–5 cm) thick. Viewed head-on they are almost invisible. From the side they are conspicuous, with a range of bars, patterns, and colors. Imperial angelfish, among the most handsome, sport an attractive mixture of blue, amber, yellow, and gold.

These are not camouflage colors. If the fish are trying to hide, any skin diver will tell them that, at least to human eyes, they fail gloriously. More probably the strong colors and patterns help every fish species to recognize its own kind unerringly, even in cloudy water or poor light. Angelfish lay their eggs in nests among the rocks, which both parents guard. When the young emerge, the first moving objects they see are their parents. So they have good reason to recognize their own species for the rest of their lives.

Monarch butterfly WARNING COLORS

Butterflies are seemingly fragile and delicate creatures, with wings all too easily crushed and broken, and bodies vulnerable to every wind that blows. Yet here are butterflies, only 4 inches (10 cm) across, that every autumn travel the length of North America, from Canada and the northern United States, to winter in California, Mexico, and Florida.

Monarchs are among the toughest butterflies, and the most easily recognizable, because they are patterned on both sides of their wings. Their caterpillars, almost 2 inches (5 cm) long, are strikingly colored with orange, yellow, and black stripes. Both butterflies and caterpillars are poisonous to predators. The caterpillars gather their poison from the sap of the milkweeds on which they feed. It is harmless to them, but causes vomiting or death in predators. A bird that eats a monarch caterpillar or butterfly is likely to find it tastes very bad, and vomit it up a few minutes later. If it does not, the bird will absorb the poison and die.

Of course, this will be of no help to the individual caterpillar or butterfly that has been swallowed. But a bird learns quickly to avoid actions that bring unpleasant results. The experience may teach it to leave monarch butterflies or caterpillars alone, so monarchs as a species reap the benefits.

— Fiddler crab DEMENTED MUSICIAN

Crabs come in a range of sizes, from monsters over 3 feet (1 m) across to tiny pea crabs of less than 1 inch (2.5 cm). Fiddler crabs are at the smaller end of the range. This male crab from South America is about 2 inches (5 cm) across the shell, with a "fiddle" — one vastly enlarged claw, held under the chin like a violin — of matching size. Females are of similar size, but without fiddles. They live in shallow intertidal waters of tropical seas and estuaries. At low tide they cover the sand or mud in thousands, males as well as females, each in the mouth of a tiny burrow just out of reach of its neighbors. There they scrape the surface for tiny animals and plants, a food source that is renewable with every change of tide.

Fiddler crabs neither scrape nor pluck their fiddles, but wave them rhythmically in the air, sometimes clicking simultaneously, like an orchestra of demented musicians. Different species wave in different ways, but their waves generally signal "keep-away" to other males and "come-hither" to females, and perhaps help to stimulate the females toward breeding condition. The fiddles are not only a show-off. Occasionally the males use them for fighting, hurling each other around in a kind of stylized "crab-karate."

Hippopotamus BARING ITS TEETH

Though the name "hippopotamus" means "river horse," there is little of the horse about the average hippo. "River pig" would more closely describe its biological kinship and way of life. Hippos live in swamps, reed beds, and rivers of tropical Africa. During hot sunny days they lie submerged, with eyes, ears, and nostrils above the surface, or in muddy wallows where they can keep their hairless hide moist. Emerging in the cool of the evening, they feed through the dark hours on grass and other riverside vegetation.

They live in herds of up to a hundred, with the females and calves together in a central area, the males scattered individually around the edges, each in a small territory of its own. Theirs is an easy life, based on constructive idleness. Females and calves seldom quarrel, and males find little to quarrel about. Should a boundary be overstepped and trouble arise, males find it easier to show off their weapons of conflict rather than put them to use. This wide gaping might be a yawn. It also displays a collection of formidable incisors and canine teeth, which the hippo *will* use in a fierce and bloody fight — if he can stay awake long enough.

Poison arrow frogs BEACONS IN THE FOREST

Here are three frogs, each less than 2 inches (5 cm) across, from the tropical forests of South and Central America. Though sometimes found on the ground, they are really tree frogs, living in damp moss, bathing, and fishing for insect larvae in tiny pools in the rough bark, and carrying their eggs and tadpoles in capsules on their backs.

By jungle rules, a frog is a tidy morsel of food for many kinds of lizards, birds, or monkeys. Most frogs fare better by matching their backgrounds closely, but these glow like tiny beacons. Some say it is because they are poisonous — the bright color is a warning to predators. It probably warns that, like many other frogs and toads, they taste nasty, as well as being poisonous. That is a lesson quickly learned, and not easily forgotten.

That they contain poison is certain. The yellow one in the middle is poisonous to touch, and from the two others native Indians extract a few drops of strong nerve poison, which they paint on the tips of their arrows. Now the jungle rules are reversed, and predators become prey. A lizard, bird, or monkey even scratched by a frog-poisoned arrow dies within minutes.

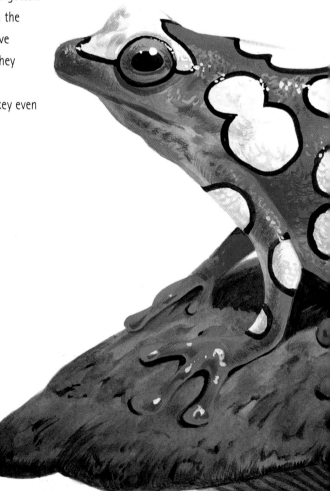

Poison arrow frogs come in many different colors.

Index CREATURES AND FEATURES